CONTE

MW01056601

Understanding
Chord Progressions
for Guitar

by Arnie Berle
Use the chords in this book to play most any song.
Get to know the most popular progressions in
folk, blues, pop, and jazz.

Amsco Publications
New York • London • Sydney

Gibson L4 on cover owned by Scot Arch
Cover photograph by William Draffen
Interior design and layout by Len Vogler

Copyright © 1995 by Amsco Publications
A Division of Music Sales Corporation, New York

Order No. AM 931250
US International Standard Book Number: 0.8256.1488.0
UK International Standard Book Number: 0.7119.5126.8

Exclusive Distributors:
Music Sales Corporation
257 Park Avenue South, New York New York 10010 USA
Music Sales Limited
8/9 Frith Street, London W1V 5TZ England
Music Sales Pty. Limited
120 Rothschild Street, Rosebery, Sydney, NSW 2018, Australia

Printed in the United States of America by
Vicks Lithograph and Printing Corporation

INTRODUCTION

The purpose of this book is to provide the student with an easy, direct, and practical approach to the study of chords and progressions and their application to song accompaniment.

Chords

Although there are literally hundreds and hundreds of chord forms that one can play, the truth is that most of these chord forms are simply embellished variations of a few more basic chord forms. In other words, it is not really necessary to learn all of the chord forms that are shown in so many chord books. With the chords shown in this book you should be able to play most any song. When you feel comfortable with what you learn in this book, you can add to these basic chords any of the hundreds of embellished chords to dress up your progressions.

Progressions

Chords, by themselves, have about as much value as the words in a dictionary. Words take on more meaning when they are used in sentences, and chords take on more meaning when they are used in progressions. Just as a story is made up of sentences, the harmony to a song is made up of progressions. In this book you will learn how to make up, and dress up, some of the more frequently used progressions heard in folk, blues, pop, and jazz.

CHORDS OF REST

Chords of rest are chords that offer a feeling of finality, a sense of having "arrived." These chords are used at the end of a song, but they also may begin a song—and they may be heard in the middle of a song as a sort of rest stop. Playing through the chords of a song is like taking a round-trip from home. You begin your trip from home, you may make several comforting rest stops along the way, and then you return home.

Let's begin by looking at the most basic rest chord there is, the *major chord*. Using a common musical shorthand, this chord is referred to as the *I chord* since it is built from the first note of any major scale. The diagrams below show two ways of fingering a major chord. One fingering shows the *root* (the letter-name) of the chord played on the 6th string and the other fingering shows the root of the chord played on the 5th string. These chord-forms are called *bar chords*, the "bar" being the first finger laid over two or more strings. These forms are most often used by rock and folk guitarists.

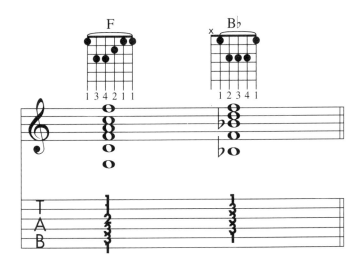

These are *moveable* chord forms and should be played up the fingerboard. The diagram below shows the letter-name of each fret along the 6th and 5th strings. Memorize the name of each chord at each fret.

fret	I	II	III	IV	V	VI	VII	VIII	IX	X	XI	XII
5th string	B♭	B	C	C♯	D	E♭	E	F	F♯	G	A♭	A
6th string	F	F♯	G	A♭	A	B♭	B	C	C♯	D	E♭	E

CHORDS OF MOVEMENT

Chords of movement are chords that generate a feeling of motion—they want to move forward, they create tension that demands resolution.

Below are two kinds of movement chords. The *dominant 7 chord* is built from the fifth note of the major scale and is referred to as the *V chord*. The *minor 7 chord* is built from the second note of the major scale and is referred to as the *II chord*. Play these chords up the fingerboard and memorize their letter-name at each fret.

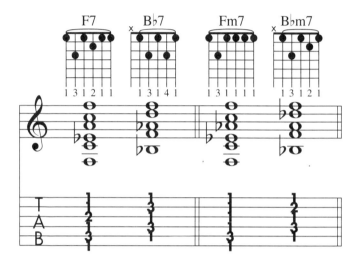

Another very valuable form for the dominant 7 chord (V chord) is shown below. Notice that this chord form has two roots, one on the 2nd string and one of the 5th string.

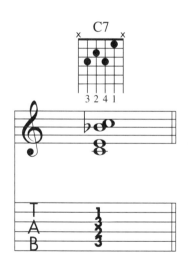

fret	I	II	III	IV	V	VI	VII	VIII	IX	X	XI	XII
2nd string	C	C♯	D	E♭	E	F	F♯	G	A♭	A	B♭	B
5th string	—	—	C	C♯	D	E♭	E	F	F♯	G	A♭	A

7

THE V-I PROGRESSION

Now put some of the chords you've learned into use as we play some very simple but important progressions. The *V-I progression* is a perfect example of a chord of movement moving to a chord of rest. Below are two examples of how to play the same progression but on different parts of the fingerboard.

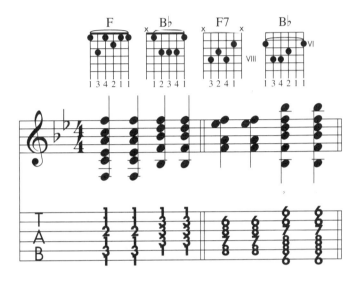

Here are two more examples of how to play the V-I progression in another key.

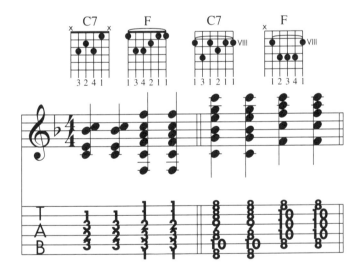

THE II-V PROGRESSION

The most often used progression in all music from pop to rock to jazz is the *II-V progression*. Placing the II in front of the V increases the tension, the feeling of movement. Sometimes the V is followed by the I and sometimes you might play a whole series of II-V chords before finally resolving to I. Below are two examples of how to play the same II-V progression.

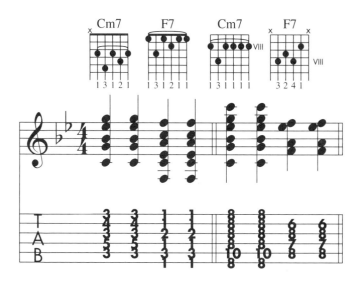

Here again are two ways to play the II-V progression in another key.

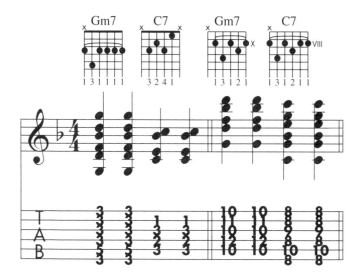

THE II-V-I PROGRESSION

Almost any time you see a II-V chord sequence, it will be followed by the I chord. The II-V chords set up the tension, and the I chord releases the tension. Below is an example of II-V-I in the key of B♭. It should be practiced in all keys.

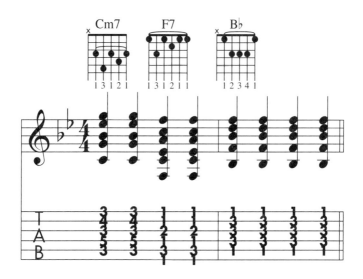

Here is the II-V-I progression in the key of F.

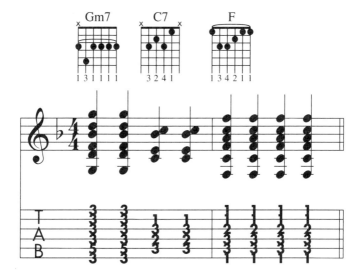

THE I-IV-V BLUES PROGRESSION

A very common progression in blues, rock, and jazz is the I-IV-V progression in the form known as the *twelve-bar blues*. Below are the chords to be used for this standard blues progression in the key of G. Notice that the IV chord is the chord built on the fourth note of the major scale and that it's another major chord like the I chord.

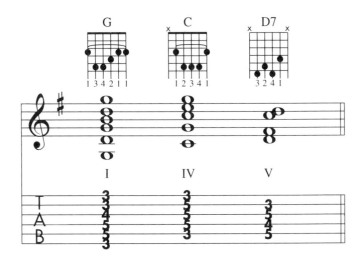

The blues is a twelve-measure form. Below you can see how the I, IV, and V chords are placed within the twelve measures. Each slash mark (/) represents one beat. Play the chord once for each slash mark.

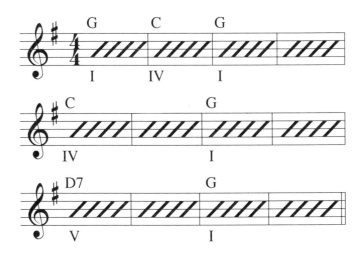

Variations on the Blues Progression

The blues progression offers many possibilities for variations. Here is one example.

- Play all I and IV chords as dominant 7 chords. These chords give a "bluesy" or funky effect.

- Use II chords to create a II-V-I sequence.

Here are the chord forms we will use in this variation.

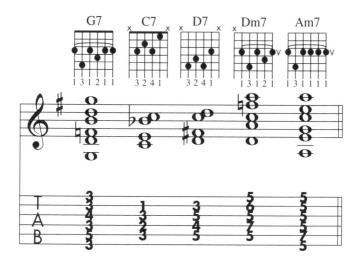

Here is the variation on the blues progression.

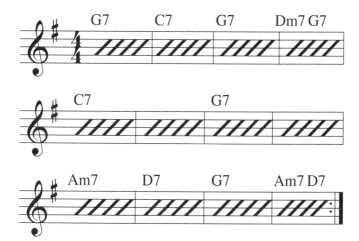

12

THE I-VI-II-V PROGRESSION

This progression is heard over and over again in those "oldies but goodies" tunes. The VI chord is another minor 7 chord built on the sixth note of the major scale.

Here is the I-VI-II-V progression in the key of F.

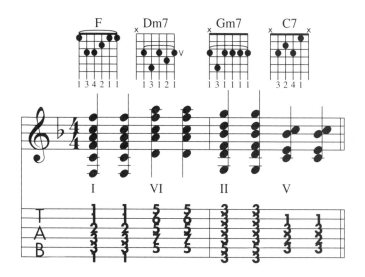

Here is the I-VI-II-V progression in the key of C.

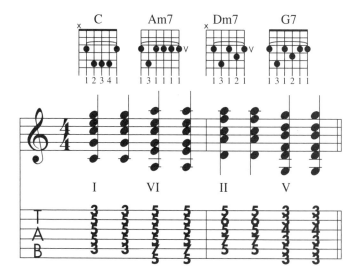

SOME JAZZIER CHORDS

If you want to sound a bit hipper or more
sophisticated, then these are the chords for you.
Notice that another form of the I chord is the *major
6*. Learn these chords up the fingerboard.

I Chords

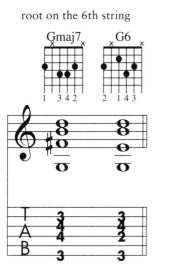

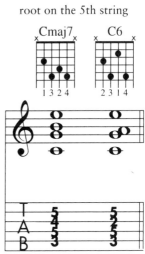

V Chords

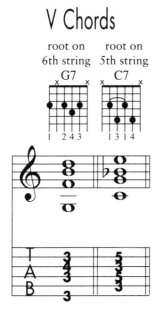

II Chords

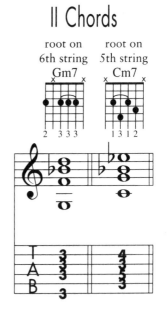

PLAYING THE II-V PROGRESSION WITH JAZZ CHORDS

Here is the II-V progression played with our new jazz chords plus one old form of the dominant 7. Notice how playing the same chords in a different position on the fingerboard gives a new flavor to the same basic progression.

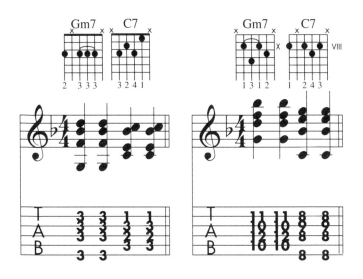

Here is another example of the II-V progression in another key played in two different positions on the fingerboard.

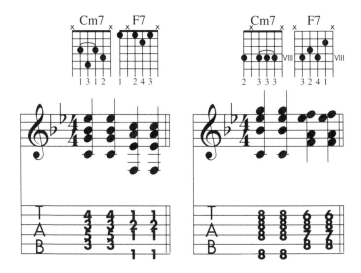

II-V-I WITH JAZZ CHORDS

Here is the ever-popular II-V-I progression using our new jazz chords. Notice that the major 6 chord is another form of the I chord and that its use is optional.

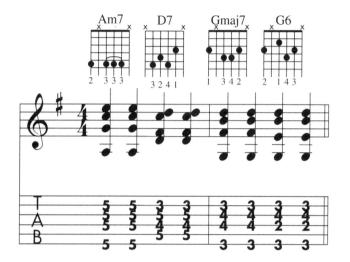

Here is another way to play the II-V-I progression in a new key.

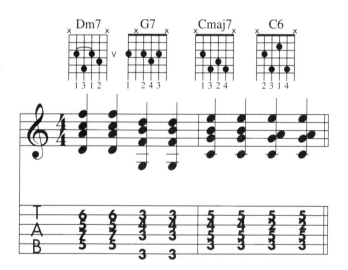

The above progressions should be played all over the fingerboard in all keys.

THE I-VI-II-V PROGRESSION WITH JAZZ CHORDS

This progression, played earlier with bar chords, is used in so many different ways that you should try to play it in all keys all over the fingerboard.

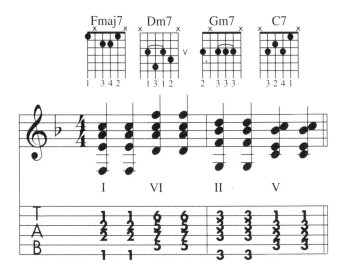

Here is another example of this progression.

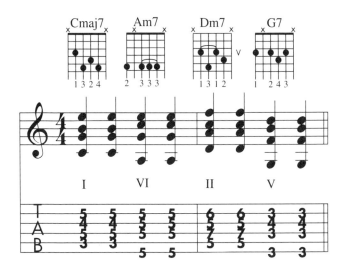

THE CYCLE

In the progression you just played, Cmaj7-Am7-Dm7-G7, notice that the roots of the Am7-Dm7-G7 move down a perfect fifth with each new chord: A down to D down to G. This movement of the roots of chords down a perfect fifth is referred to as *the cycle*.

Each of the following letters represent the roots of possible chords. They may be all major 7s, all minor 7s, all dominant 7s, or any combination of these qualities.

C F B♭ E♭ A♭ D♭ G♭ B E A D G C
(C♯)(F♯)

The most common example of the cycle is the II-V-I progression. Below is another example of cycle movement. The progression is taken from the great standard "All the Things You Are" by Jerome Kern. It is a VI-II-V-I progression.

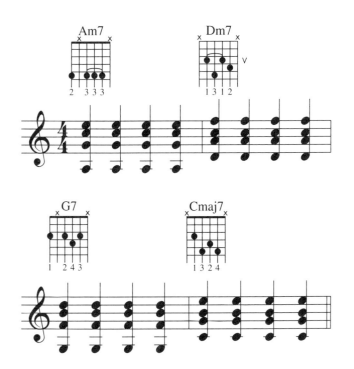

EXTENDING AND ALTERING THE I CHORD

All chords may be extended or altered in order to create more interesting tonal colors. Since the I chord is a chord of resolution, it does not take too well to alterations that add tension. Below are examples of extended I major chords.

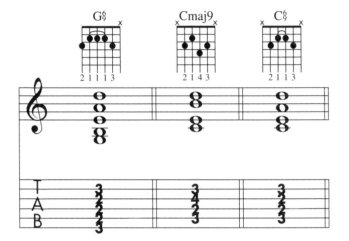

EXTENDING AND ALTERING THE V CHORD

Since the V chords create tension, a feeling of movement, they can take altered notes as well as extensions. Here are some examples.

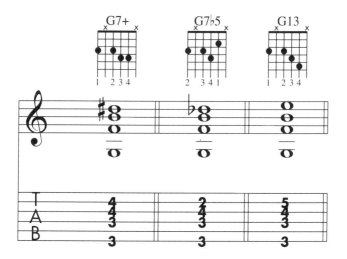

Here are more examples of altered chords, continuing with our extended and altered V dominant chords.

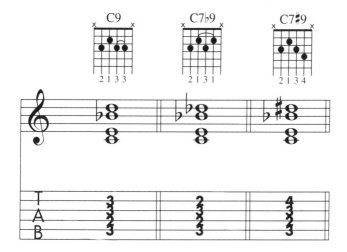

EXTENDING AND ALTERING THE II MINOR CHORDS

The minor chords don't lend themselves to many extensions or alterations but the following examples are rather common.

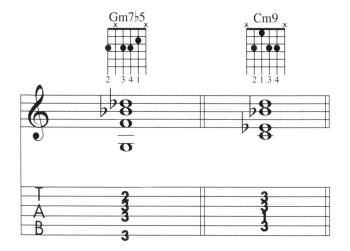

DRESSING UP YOUR PROGRESSIONS

When you extend or alter a basic chord you are dressing it up—or, in musical terminology, *embellishing* it. Embellished chords create more interesting and colorful progressions. Here is the familiar II-V-I progression in C with embellishments added to all three chords. Notice how these embellishments create a smooth, chromatic melody.

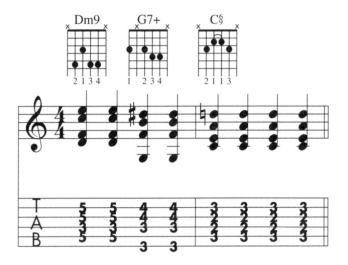

In this next example of an embellished II-V-I progression notice the new form for the C6 chord. This is another moveable form and should be practiced up the fingerboard.

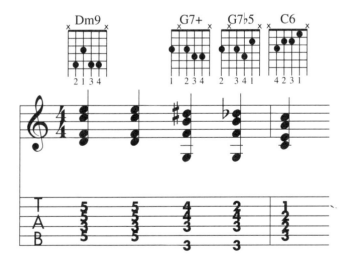

Here is another example, continuing with our embellished II-V-I progressions.

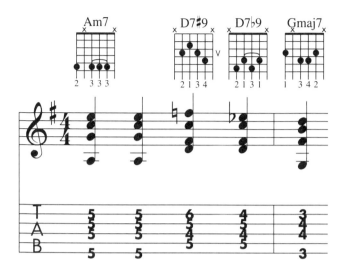

Here is another embellished II-V-I progression with an altered II chord (IIm7b5).

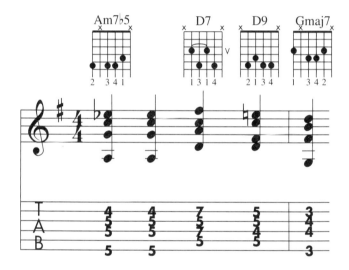

Chord Substitution
The Tritone Substitution

Another way to dress up a bland progression is
through the use of *chord substitutes*. Any dominant
7 may be replaced with another dominant 7 whose
root is three whole-tones above the root of the
original chord. This is called a *tritone subsitution*.

original progression

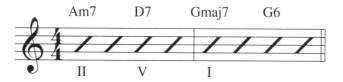

with tritone substitution

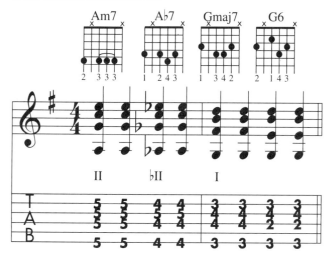

Notice how the tritone substitution creates a
descending chromatic bassline. It's easy to remember
the tritone substitution for a V chord because it will
always be the dominant 7 chord that is one half-step
above the I chord. You can think of it as the ♭II7
chord.

Changing Chord Quality

Another type of substitution results when you change the quality of a chord—major, minor, dominant, etc.—while the root remains the same.

original progression

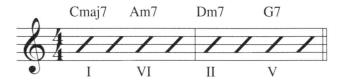

with chord-quality substitution

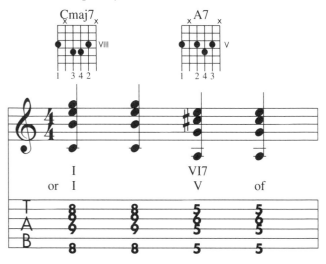

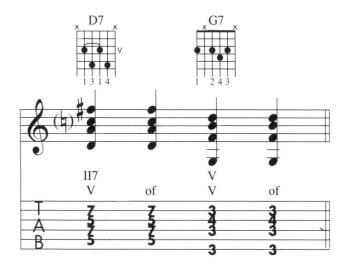

By changing the minor 7 chords to dominant 7 chords we increase the level of tension making the resolution to the I more satisfying. The second line of Roman numerals shows a different way to analyze this progression: Think of the A7 as the V of D7, and the D7 as the V of G7.

Substituting the III Chord for the I Chord

In the key of C, the III chord is Em7 and the notes are E G B D. The I chord is Cmaj7 and the notes are C E G B. Since three of the notes in Em7 are the same as three notes of the Cmaj7, we can substitute the III chord for the I.

original progression

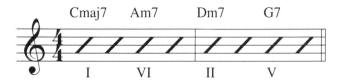

with III-for-I and chord-quality substitution

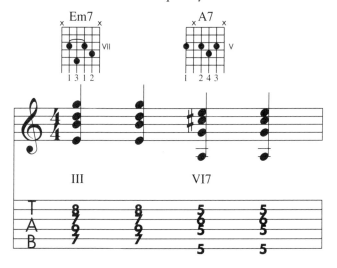

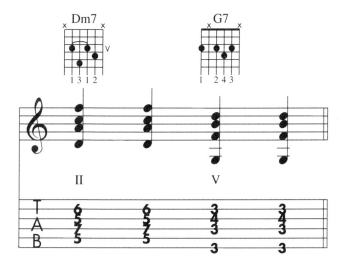

By substituting III for I and changing the quality of the VI to a dominant 7, we have set up a series of II-V chords.

Combining Substitutions

By combining some of the substitutions—III chord for the I, tritone, and changing chord quality—we arrive at the following new progression.

original progression

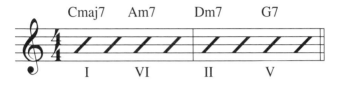

substitute progression

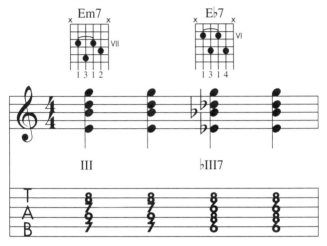

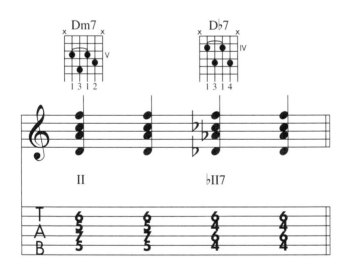

Using these substitutions, you create a descending chromatic bassline. This is much more interesting and colorful than the original I-VI-II-V progression.

CHORDS WITH THE 5TH IN THE BASS

Up until now all the chords have been played with the roots in the bass (lowest note). Now let's see how some of these chords may be played with the 5th in the bass.

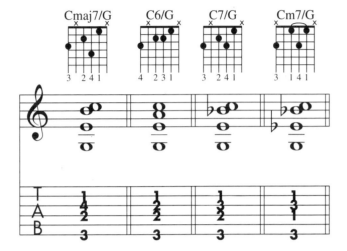

CHORDS WITH THE ♭5 IN THE BASS

Here are two commonly used chords with the ♭5 in the bass.

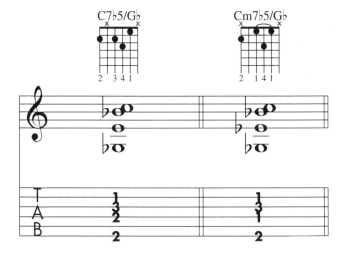

MOVING LINES IN THE BASS

By using combinations of unaltered chords and altered chords you can create some more interesting and colorful progressions with some nice moving lines. Listen carefully to the following progressions and play them all over the fingerboard. Hear the moving line in the bass in this progression.

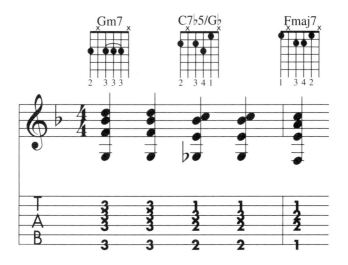

In this next progression, listen to the moving lines in both the bass and the top line.

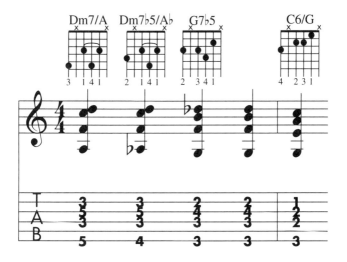

MOVING LINES IN THE TOP VOICE

Moving lines on the top of the chord tend to stand out more clearly than moving lines on the inside of the chords.

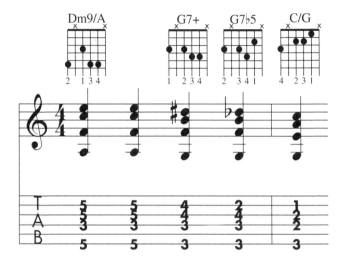

Here is another example of a moving line played on the top of the chords.

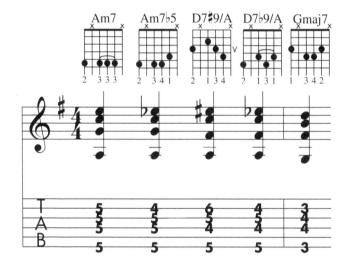

THE HARMONIZED MAJOR SCALE

When you harmonize each step of a major scale, the resulting chords are referred to as *diatonic chords*. The following scale is based on chords whose roots are on the 6th string.

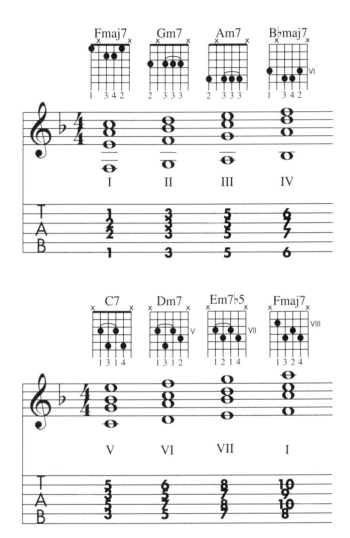

For a more in-depth study of harmonized scales see *Chords and Progressions for Jazz and Pop Guitar* by Arnie Berle.

IMPROVING A WEAK PROGRESSION
Fill-In Chords

Fill-in chords are used to add interest or motion to a weak or static progression. These fill-in chords are usually taken from the harmonized scale. When a I chord is held for a long period of time you can use combinations of the II and III chords to strengthen the progression. Below are two examples of how this might be done.

original progression

fill-in no. 1

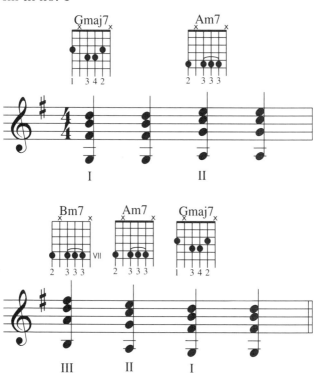

fill-in no. 2

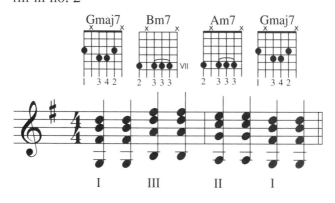

Chromatic Passing Chords

A chromatic passing chord is a chord that is not in the harmonized scale but may be used to connect any two chords of the scale that are a whole step apart.

original progression

with chromatic passing chords

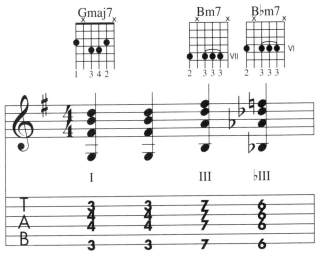

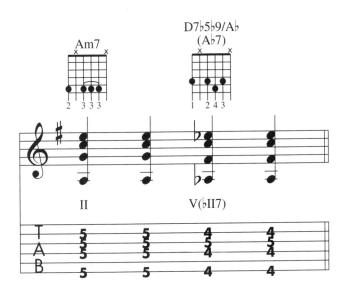

Notice that the II chord is placed in front of the V chord. II may always be placed in front of a V chord. Notice also that the altered D7 chord D7♭9♭5/A♭, produces an A♭7 chord which is the tritone substitution (♭II7) for the V chord.

34

The Diminished 7 Chord

The *diminished 7 chord* is formed by lowering the 3rd, 5th, and 7th of any dominant 7 chord by one half-step. It is used as a linking chord or a passing chord between two chords a whole step apart. Below are two fingerings for the diminished 7 chord.

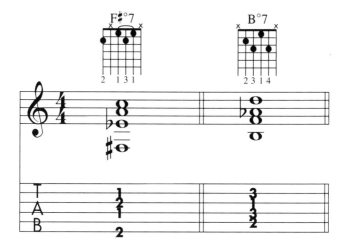

Because each of the notes that make up the diminished 7 chord is equally distant from its neighbors, any of the notes in the chord may be considered the root of the chord.

The diminished 7 may be used as a passing chord connecting the I chord to the II chord.

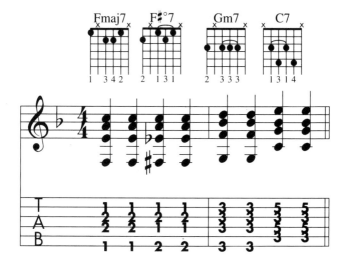

When a I chord is held for two measures, the diminished 7 may be used as a passing or connecting chord between the II and the III chords. (Remember that the III chord serves as a substitute for the I chord.)

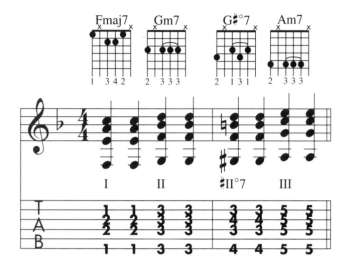

Here's how to play the same progression in C from the 5th string.

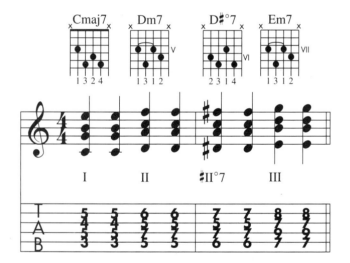

When a I chord is held for a prolonged period of time (three or four measures), the diminished 7 chord may be used in the following manner. Since the III chord is a substitution for the I chord we can move scalewise up the harmonized scale by using the diminished 7 chord as a passing chord until we reach the III chord.

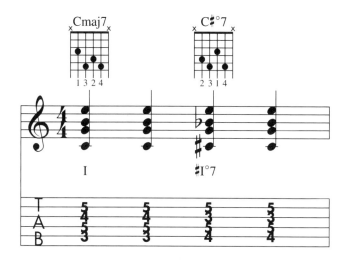

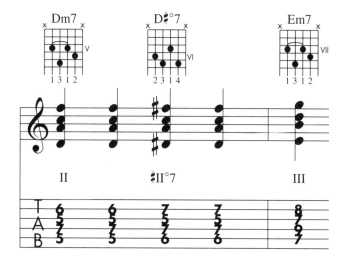

THE HALF-STEP-APPROACH CHORD

Any chord may be approached by another chord which is a half step higher or lower. The approach chord is generally, but not always, the same quality and form as the chord that follows. See below how this is applied to the I-VI-II-V progression.

original progression

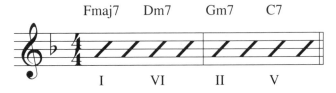

played with approach chords

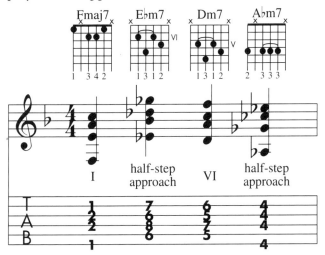

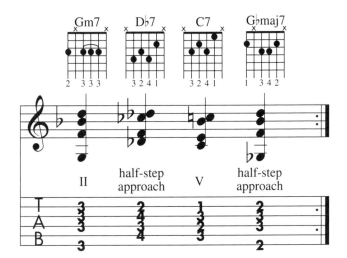

In order to add some interest and color to our I-VI-II-V progression let's add some extensions and altered notes to change the quality of some of the chords.

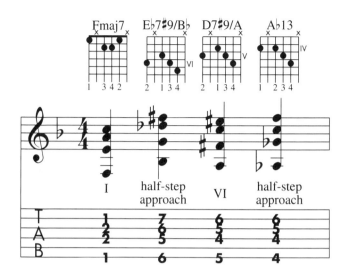

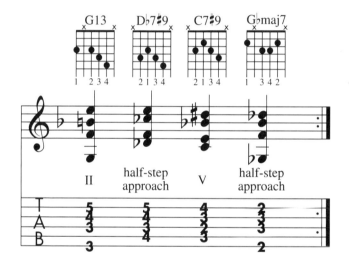

MODULATIONS

Moving from one key to another key is called
modulation. The simplest and most direct way to
modulate is to play the II-V chords of the new key.

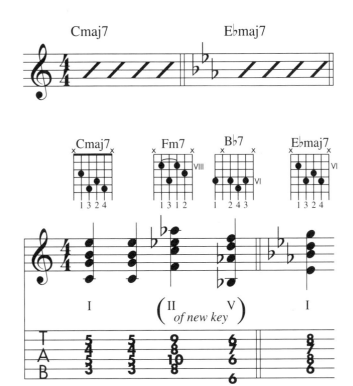

In moving from the key of C to the key of D you
can "walk" up to the Em7 (II of D) by going from
Cmaj7 to Dm7 to Em7 to A7 to Dmaj7.

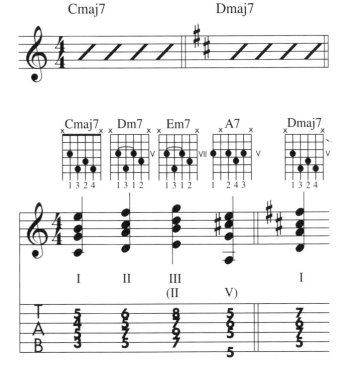

INTRODUCTIONS

Introductions are used to set the mood, the tempo, and most importantly, the feeling of key. The important thing to remember is that the first chord of the tune must be prepared by its II-V chords. For example, if the first chord of the tune is a I chord, then you must prepare it by playing the II-V of that I chord. However, you might want to start your introduction further back. In that case you can play our old friend the I-VI-II-V progression leading to the I of the song.

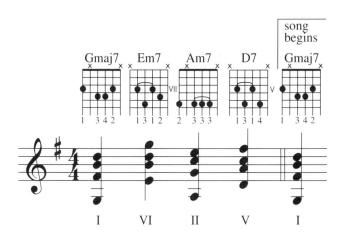

Another technique is to *backcycle;* that is, go as far back on the cycle as you want and play a series of II-V chords until you resolve to the I chord of the tune.

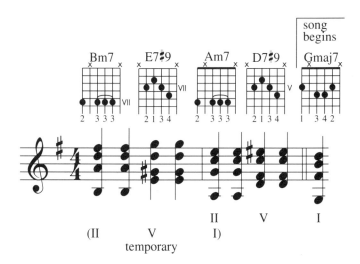

When the first chord of the song is a II chord—as in "Satin Doll" by Duke Ellington—the principle still works. Think of the II chord as a temporary I and precede it with a II-V. To stretch it out, you can think of the new II chord again as a temporary I and play the II-V of the temporary I.

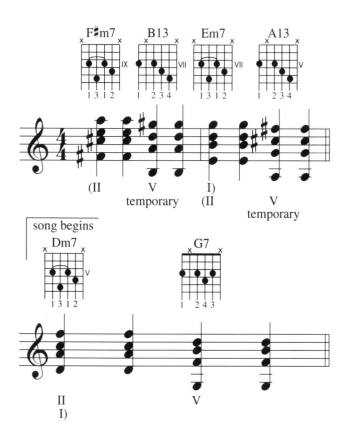

By using the ♭II substitution (tritone substitution) for the V chords, we come up with the following. Again, listen to the moving line in the top voice of the chords, as well as in the bass.

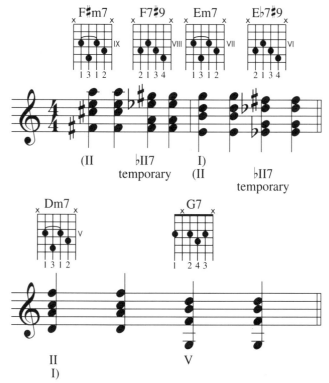

Tag Endings

A *tag* ending is an extension of a song or a delaying of the final ending of the song. The most common method of delaying the ending is by replacing the final I chord with a substitute chord, usually the III chord and then moving through the cycle until you arrive at the final I chord.

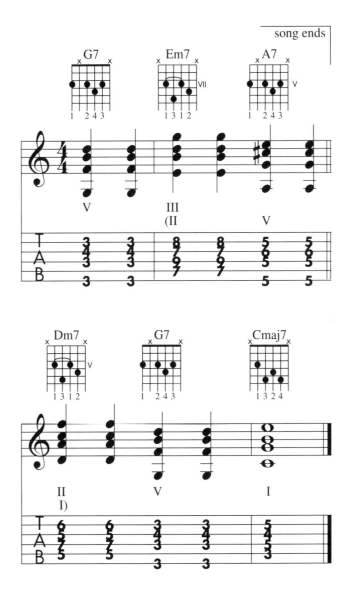

Notice how the III chord replaces the original I chord and then moves through the cycle finally coming to an end on the I chord.

Here is a variation on the tag ending you just played. Notice that the E♭9 is a tritone substitution for the A7 chord and the A♭m7-D♭7♭9 is a tritone substitution for the Dm7-G7 that normally precedes the I chord.

Another effective ending is to play a series of chords that keep the root of the I chord in the top voice. Note the new chord forms.

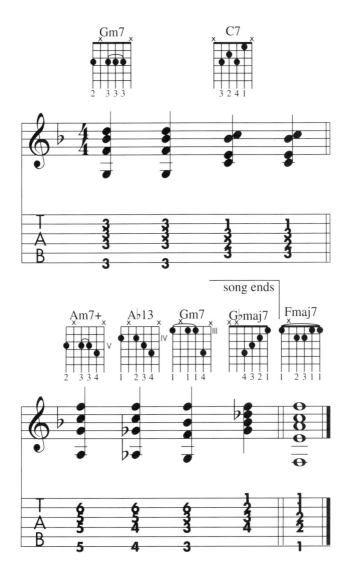

Notice that the Am7+ is a III chord which is the substitution for the Fmaj7 which is the I chord. And then we descend chromatically to the I chord.

In this last example, we use the B♭13 as a tritone substitution for the III chord (which is another substitution for the I chord). Then we proceed through the cycle with each chord containing the root of the I chord as a common tone. We finally descend a half step to the I chord.

original progression

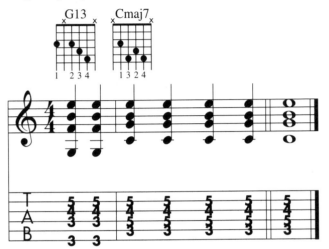

tag ending

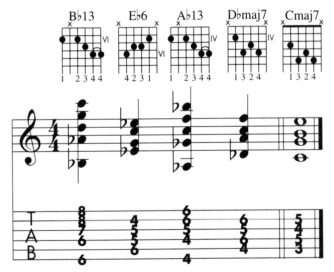

THE TURNAROUND

A *turnaround* is a one- or two-measure progression that comes at the end of a section of music and sends you back to the top. Turnarounds are commonly found in the last two measures of a blues progression. Here is a basic turnaround.

To add harmonic interest to this basic progression we can put the II chord in front of the V.

To add still further harmonic interest we can put the VI chord in front of the II chord.

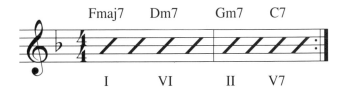

Notice that we arrive back at the I-VI-II-V progression. To this progression we can now add extensions, alterations, and substitutions to create more interest.

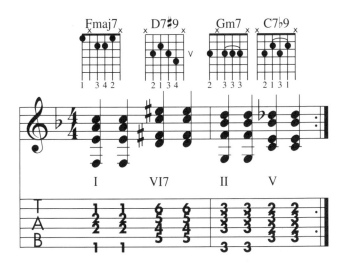

BACK TO THE BLUES

The blues form gives us an excellent opportunity to make use of all the things we've learned so far. Let's start with a basic blues progression as used by jazz players.

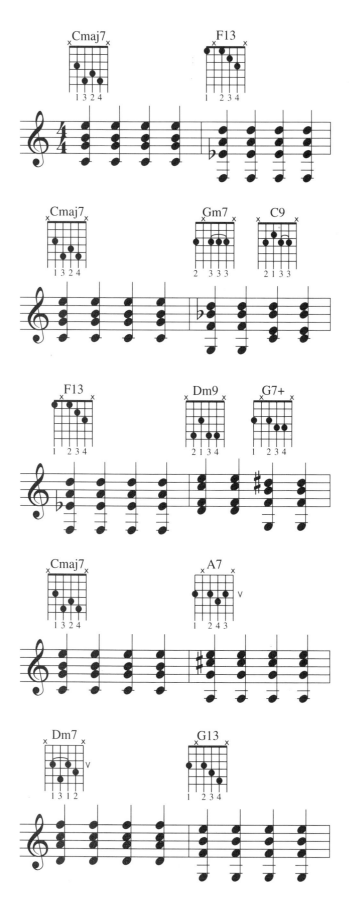

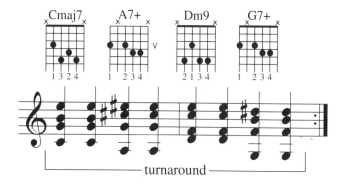

Bebop Blues Variation

Here is another variation on the blues. This was used by the bebop players of the 1940s. Notice the extended series of II-V sequences leading to the IV chord in measure 5.

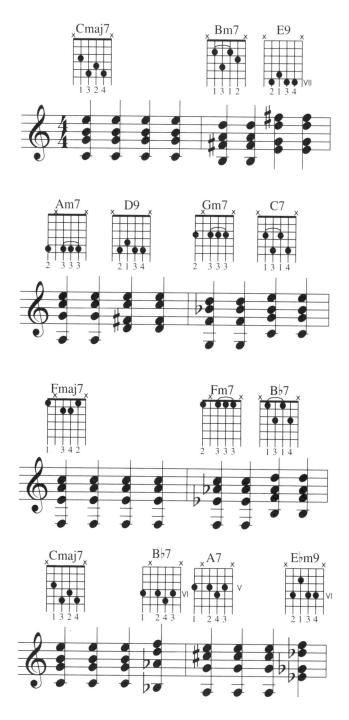

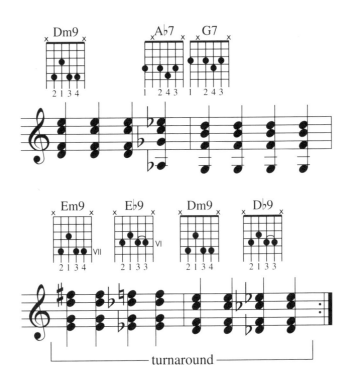

turnaround

Another Blues Variation

Here is one more example of a blues progression variation. This one uses several of the chord sequences and substitutions you have learned so far.

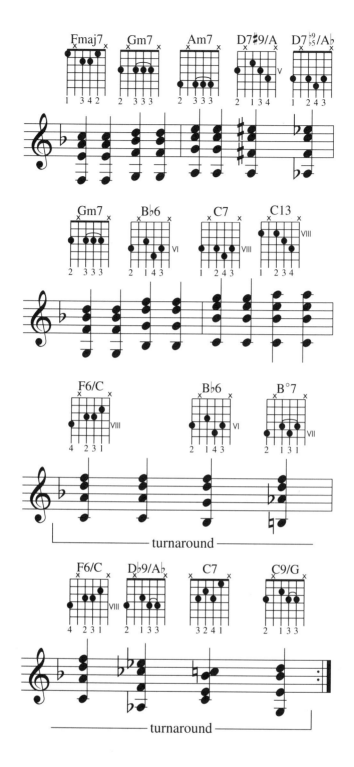

CHORD SUSPENSIONS

Suspensions are often used to delay resolution to the I chord. The suspended note is usually the fourth note of the scale which replaces the third of the chord. Below are two examples.

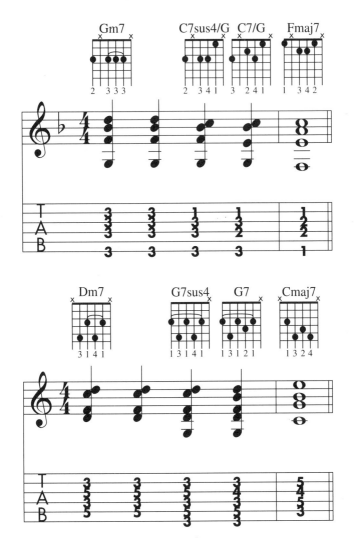

PLAYING THE MINOR II-V-I

The following II-V-I sequence is useful for songs written in a minor key.

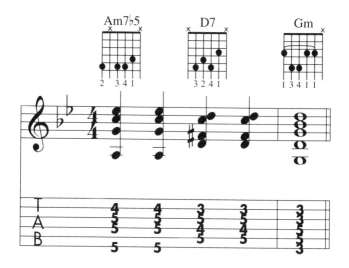

It could also be played like this.

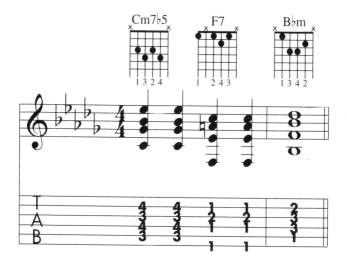

Minor II-V-I Variations

Use the following chord forms for a minor II-V-I to create a stronger feeling of the minor key.

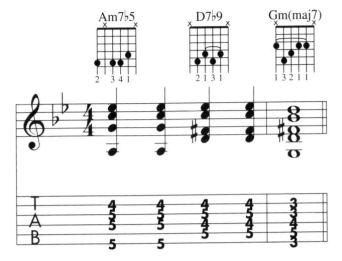

Here is still another way to play a minor II-V-I progression.

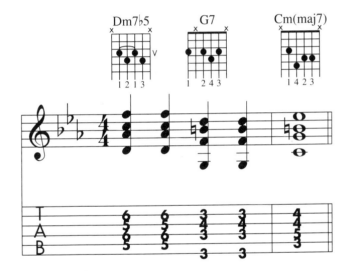

THE IM-IM(MAJ7)-IM7-IM6

This sequence is found in such tunes as "My Funny Valentine," "Michelle," "More," and "What Are You Doing the Rest of Your Life?" Notice how the following chord forms suggest an interesting moving line played on the 4th string.

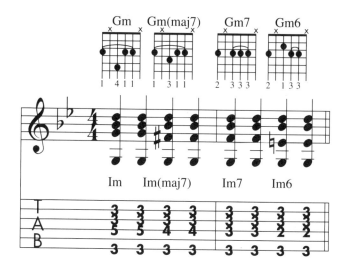

Here is another way to play this progression, this time with the moving line on the 2nd string.

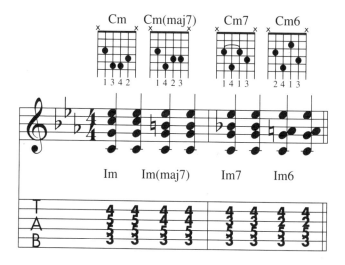

Im-Im(maj7)-Im7-Im6 as a Substitute for II-V

The Im-Im(maj7)-Im7-Im6 chords may also be used as a substitution for the II-V chords in a major key.

original progression

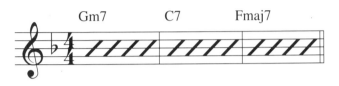

with substitution

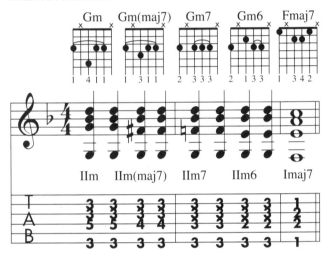

original progression

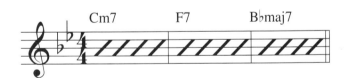

with substitution

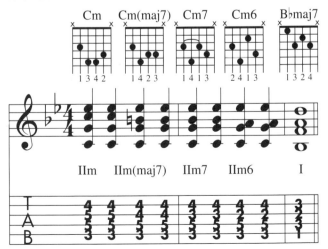

THREE-NOTE CHORDS

Three-note chords are almost always played on the 6th, 4th, and 3rd strings. The notes that give the chord its quality are always played. These notes are the 3rd and 7th of the chord. The 5th or, in some cases, the root may be omitted from the chord. Here are some of the most frequently played three-string chords.

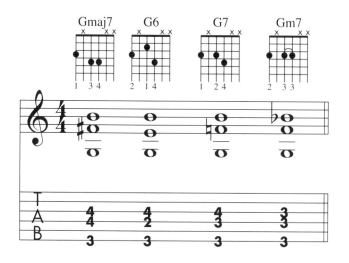

Notice that the following chords all have the 5th in the bass. You can also put the root in the bass by substituting the optional note for the lowest note in each chord.

○ = optional bass note

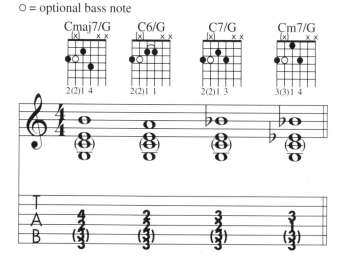

PLAYING THE II-V-I PROGRESSION WITH THREE-NOTE CHORDS

Listen to the interesting moving line you can get in the top notes of these chords.

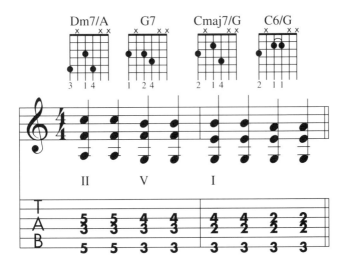

Here is a II-V-I progression with a different set of chords.

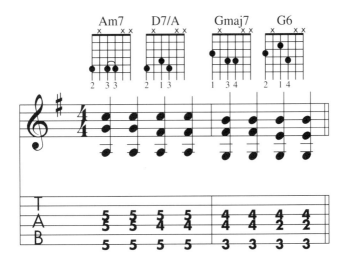

II-V Chords in Cycle Movement

Note that all the V chords in this backcycling progression are played with the root on the 5th string. Listen for the descending line played on the 4th string.

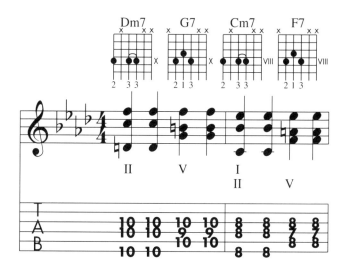

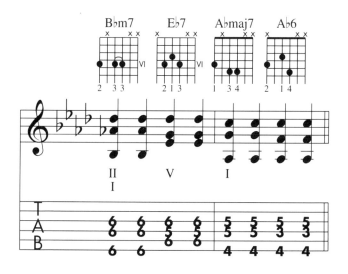

The following series of II-V chords resolve to the I chord and have a descending line in the top voice.

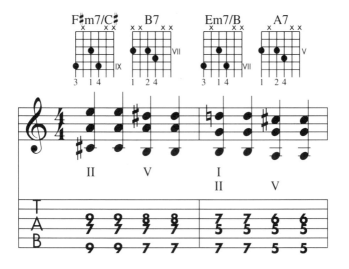

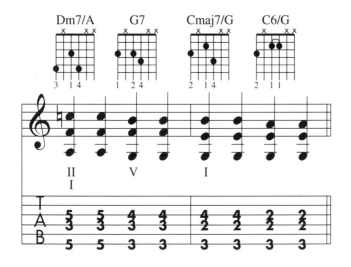

Notice that all II chords may be played with the root on the 5th string if you prefer.

THREE-NOTE CHORD FORMS FOR Im-Im(maj7)-Im7-Im6

When the Im-Im(maj7)-Im7-Im6 chords appear in a tune it is a good idea to bring out the moving line that is suggested by the chord symbols. The following series of three-note chord forms allows the moving line to be heard in the lowest voice.

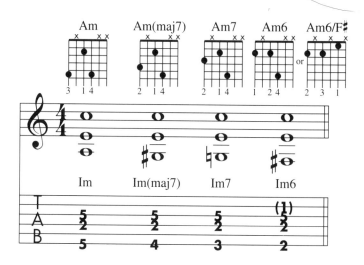

In this next series of chord forms the moving line is placed in the top voice.

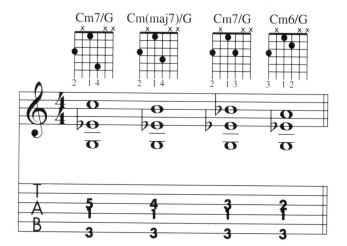

THE IM-IM+-IM6 CHORD SEQUENCE

The minor–minor augmented–minor 6 chord sequence has a number of uses. Here is a practical series of chord forms.

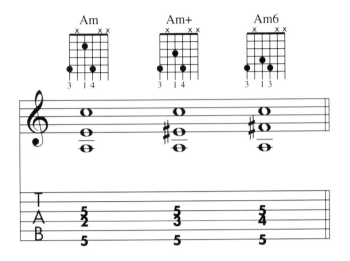

The above chord sequence may be used any time a minor chord appears. The example below shows the sequence in a II-V situation.

original progression

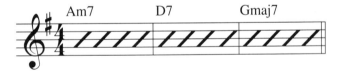

with substitution

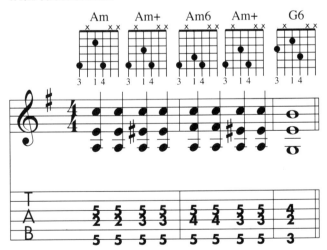

Im-Im+-Im6 as a Substitute for a Dominant 7

For a V-I progression you may play the minor–minor augmented–minor 6 sequence in place of the V chord. Just start on the minor chord whose root is the 5th of the V chord. For example, to substitute for an F7, start on Cm.

original progression

with substitution

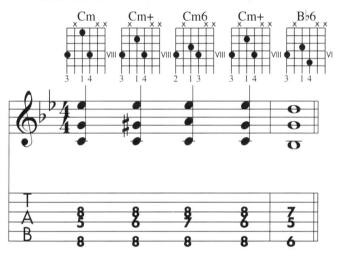

Finally, the same sequence may be used to add interest and movement when a major chord is held for two or more measures. Start the sequence on the minor chord whose root is a major 3rd up from the root of the major chord.

original progression

with substitution

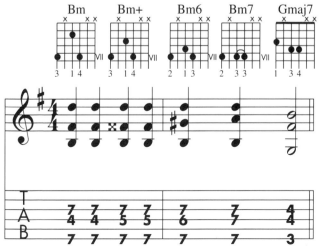

Guitar Compact Reference Books

Here are other great titles in this series that you will want to add to your collection:

GUITAR

The Advanced Guitar Case Chord Book
by Askold Buk

68 pp AM 80227
ISBN 0.8256.1243.8
$4.95

Prepack AM 90176
$59.40

The Advanced Guitar Case Scale Book
by Darryl Winston

48 pp AM 91462
ISBN 0.8256.1370.1
$4.95

Prepack AM 91463
$59.40

Basic Blues Guitar
by Darryl Winston

56 pp AM 91281
ISBN 0.8256.1366.3
$4.95

Prepack AM 91246
$59.40

Beginning Guitar
by Artie Traum

64 pp AM 36997
ISBN 0.8256.2332.2
$4.95

Prepack AM 86997
$59.40

Beginning Rock Guitar
by Artie Traum

48 pp AM 37292
ISBN 0.8256.2444.4
$4.95

Prepack AM 37300
$59.40

The Compact Blues Guitar Chord Reference
compiled by Len Vogler

48 pp AM 91731
ISBN 0.8256.1385.X
$4.95

Prepack AM 91732
ISBN 0.8256.1386.8
$59.40

The Compact Rock Guitar Chord Reference
compiled by Len Vogler

48pp AM 91733
ISBN 0.8256.1387.6
$4.95

Prepack AM 91734
ISBN 0.8256.1388.4
$59.40

The Original Guitar Case Scale Book
by Peter Pickow

56 pp AM 76217
ISBN 0.8256.2588.2
$4.95

Prepack AM 86217
$59.40

Rock 'n' Roll Guitar Case Chord Book
by Russ Shipton

48 pp AM 28689
ISBN 0.86001.880.6
$4.95

Prepack AM 30891
$59.40

The Original Guitar Case Chord Book
by Peter Pickow

48 pp AM 35841
ISBN 0.8256.2998.5
$4.95

Prepack AM 36138
$59.40

Tuning Your Guitar
By Donald Brosnac

AM 35858
ISBN 0.8256.2180.1
$4.95

Prepack AM 85858
$59.40

BASS GUITAR

Beginning Bass Guitar
by Peter Pickow

80 pp AM 36989
ISBN 0.8256.2332.4
$4.95
Prepack AM 86989
$59.40

Beginning Bass Scales
by Peter Pickow

48 pp AM 87482
ISBN 0.8256.1342.6
$4.95

Prepack AM 90174
$59.40

Chord Bassics
by Jonas Hellborg

80 pp AM 60138
ISBN 0.8256.1058.3
$4.95

Prepack AM 80138
$59.40

Eight more Guitar Compact Reference Books available from Music Sales:

The Alternate Tunings Guide for Guitar
Beginning Rock Guitar
Beginning Slide Guitar
D. I. Y. Guitar Repair

Guitarist's Riff Diary
Manual de Acordes Para Guitarra
The Twelve-String Guitar Guide
Using Your Guitar

For further info contact your local music dealer or call: 1-800-431-7187